Mel Bay Presents

Country Gospel Piano Solos

By Gail Smith

CD Contents

1 2 3 4 5 6 7 8 9 0

Visit us on the Web at www.melbay.com — E-mail us at email@melbay.com

ABOUT THE AUTHOR

Gail Smith received her Bachelor of Fine Arts Degree from Florida Atlantic University. She is currently the National Music Chairman of the National League of American Pen Women and is a former president of the Broward County Branch. Ms. Smith is a member of the National Guild of Piano Teachers, Federation of Music Clubs, and is a member of MTNA. She has taught piano students from the age of 3 up to age 96. She has given concerts in churches and colleges across the United States and in Germany and Japan. She was the pianist of the famed Coral Ridge Presbyterian Church in Fort Lauderdale, Florida, for many years. Ms. Smith is known as an outstanding educator, composer and musicologist and shares her expertise on arranging and improvisation in workshops and conventions.

CONTENTS

O HAPPY DAY

Dedicated to my husband, Lon Smith

Edward F. Rimbault, 1854
Arr. by Gail Smith

AMAZING GRACE
Dedicated to Nicole Borror

Arr. by Gail Smith

DAY IS DYING IN THE WEST

Dedicated to Stacy Alexander

William F. Sherwin, 1877
Arr. by Gail Smith

9

STANDIN' IN THE NEED OF PRAYER

Dedicated to Gwendolyn Larkin

Arr. by Gail Smith

THE CHURCH IN THE WILDWOOD

Dedicated to Sharon McCrary

Dr. W.S. Pitts
Arr. by Gail Smith

REVIVE US AGAIN

Dedicated to Sally Smith

Arr. by Gail Smith

POWER IN THE BLOOD

Dedicated to Jeff Smith

Lewis E. Jones, 1899
Arr. by Gail Smith

JUST A CLOSER WALK

Dedicated to Dagmar May

Arr. by Gail Smith

THERE IS A FOUNTAIN
WHEN I CAN READ MY TITLE CLEAR

Dedicated to Elaine Brennan

Traditional American Melody
Arr. by Gail Smith

WHAT A FELLOWSHIP
Dedicated to Janet Stone

Anthony J. Showalter, 1887
Arr. by Gail Smith

TIS SO SWEET

Dedicated to Shannon Erisman

William J. Kirkpatrick, 1882
Arr. by Gail Smith

IN THE SWEET BY AND BY

Dedicated to Ken Carlson

Arr. by Gall Smith

THIS WORLD IS NOT MY HOME

Dedicated to Dr. Ken Wackes

Arr. by Gail Smith

I'LL FLY AWAY
Dedicated to Sue Hubble

Arr. by Gail Smith

BEYOND THE SUNSET
Dedicated to Marilyn Smith

Blanche Kerr Brock
Arr. by Gail Smith

rit.

a tempo

Great Music at Your Fingertips